A Question of Technology

What's so super about supercomputers?

and other questions about COMPUTING

Clive Gifford

WAYLAND

First published in Great Britain in 2022
by Wayland

© Hodder and Stoughton, 2022

All rights reserved

Credits:
Editors: Julia Bird; Julia Adams
Design and illustrations: Matt Lilly
Cover design: Matt Lilly

HB ISBN 978 1 5263 2000 1
PB ISBN 978 1 5263 2001 8

Printed and bound in China

MIX
Paper from responsible sources
FSC® C104740

Picture credits:

Dreamstime: Alamy: Archivio GBB 5tr;
Incamerastock 8tl; Newscom 26b.
Getty Images: Bettmann 4tc, 4bc.
Shutterstock: zentilia cover, 23tr; Diamond Galaxy 11t;
Ruth Black 14tr, 25br; Mauro Rodrigues 14b;
Robert Babczynski 16c; Cheers Group 20c;
Nerthuz with elements by NASA 22tr; S-F 29b.
Wikimedia Commons: Marcin Wichary 6b.

Every effort has been made to clear copyright.
Should there be any inadvertent omission,
please apply to the publisher for rectification

Wayland
An imprint of
Hachette Children's Group
Part of Hodder and Stoughton
Carmelite House
50 Victoria Embankment
London EC4Y 0DZ

An Hachette UK Company
www.hachette.co.uk
www.hachettechildrens.co.uk

WEST NORTHAMPTONSHIRE COUNCIL	
60000531997	
Askews & Holts	
BB	

Contents

4-5
What is a computer?

6-7
What did the first computer look like?

8-9
Who was the first coder?

10-11
Why were early computers so BIG?

12-13
Why make microchips so tiny?

14-15
Where does all my data go?

16-17
Why do computers take soooo long to start?

18-19
How does what I type reach the screen?

20-21
How do computer games know the score?

22-23
Is a bug the same as a virus?

24-25
Could a laser printer destroy the world?

26-27
What's so super about supercomputers?

28-29
Quick-fire questions

30-31
Glossary / Further reading

32
Index

What is a computer?

Computers are amazing machines that handle information known as data. This data may be photos, video, text, calculations or sounds.

INPUT is sending data or commands to the computer such as uploading a photo or typing an email. You use a keyboard, touchscreen or some other input device to do this.

PROCESSING sees the data worked on according to sets of instructions called programs or apps.

OUTPUT describes the results of the computer's work. They might be displayed on a screen or printed out, for example.

Hardware vs software

All the physical parts of the computer plus peripherals (bits connected to it, such as keyboards) are called hardware. Software are the different programs that tell computers what to do.

Computing pioneers

Dozens of tech geniuses have helped us create a world where computers, tablets and smartphones (which are handheld computers) are everywhere and make life easier, safer, and more fun!

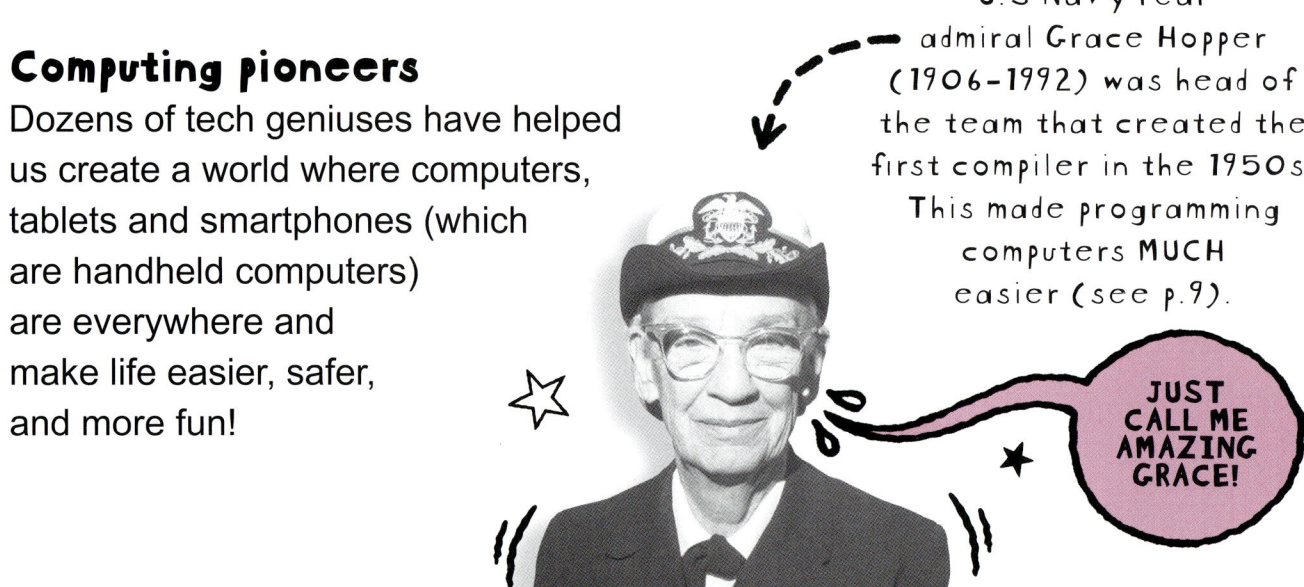

U.S Navy rear admiral Grace Hopper (1906-1992) was head of the team that created the first compiler in the 1950s. This made programming computers MUCH easier (see p.9).

JUST CALL ME AMAZING GRACE!

Bill Gates (1955-) founded Microsoft, the world's largest computer software company.

Alan Turing (1912-1954) pioneered the idea of computers that could decode and run any set of instructions.

Microsoft changed the way millions of people use computers.

YOU CAN NOW FIND ME ON THE BACK OF A UK £50 BANKNOTE!

Fujio Masuoka (1943-) invented flash memory that holds all your data in smartphones and on pen drives.

Advances in computing have changed our world. Without computers, there'd be none of the following:

Gaming ★ Music and video streaming ★ Robotics

Word processing

Online shopping

Social media Web surfing 3D printing

5

What did the first computer look like?

Not like they do today!
The first computer was invented long before plastics, silicon chips or electricity in homes. It would have been a gleaming iron and brass machine around the size of a school bus.

Computer Charlie
In the 1820s, people still used printed tables of maths sums to make their calculations. These big books were often full of errors, much to the annoyance of one Englishman, Charles Babbage (1791-1871).

He set about designing giant mechanical machines full of gears, cogs and levers called **DIFFERENCE ENGINES** to produce more accurate maths tables. Craftsmen struggled to make each Engine's 25,000 parts with enough precision and no machine was actually completed.

24,998, 24,999... ER? DRAT! 1, 2, 3...

Each tooth on each gear cog represented a different number.

In the 1830s, Babbage gave up. He had a far more ambitious idea …

By 2002, London's Science Museum completed a version of Babbage's Difference Engine No.2. At almost 3 tonnes, it weighed more than a rhino, but worked!

THAT'S HEAVY!

A True Computer

Babbage drew up detailed plans for the **ANALYTICAL ENGINE** – the first ever vision of an entire general-purpose computer. It could run different programs to perform a wide range of tasks.

Ingenious!

The 4.5-m-tall Mill was the machine's processor, performing all the maths calculations. It could repeat instructions just like processors inside a modern computer do.

The Store was the machine's memory and would have been over 6 m long. Columns of gears carried numbers from the Mill and stored them here.

Commands that make up a program were produced on cards with holes. The cards would be fed into the machine to tell it what to do.

Too hefty to work by hand, the machine would have been powered by a steam engine.

7

Who was the first coder?

> I ALSO PREDICTED THAT ONE DAY COMPUTERS WOULD DO MUCH MORE THAN JUST MATHS!

Coders write computer programs. The very first coder lived 180 years ago!

Ada, Countess of Lovelace, was a friend of Charles Babbage and a gifted mathematician. In 1843, she wrote a set of notes about Babbage's computing machines, which included the first known program – a series of instructions for a machine to solve a complex maths task.

Complex coding

Today, millions of coders write programs. Large teams work together to produce blockbuster computer games or operating systems like Windows or Android. These programs contain lots of lines of program code.

It took more than 7.7 million lines of code to program the computer game *World of Warcraft*.

A simple game or drawing program may have 500 lines of code.

Most smartphone apps are programmed with about 50,000 lines of code.

Many coders write their programs using a computer language such as Scratch, JavaScript, Python or C++. These provide lots of easy-to-use commands and instructions such as **MOVE**, **PRINT** or **REPEAT**.

Some languages, like Scratch, use colourful instruction blocks you can snap together.

```
when run
repeat 4 times
  do move forward ▼ by 100 pixels
     turn right ▼ by 144 degrees
```

Other languages, like JavaScript, are text-based.

```
for (var count = 0; count < 4; count++) {
    moveForward(100);
    turnright(144);
}
```

Zero chat

Now, your computer only understands binary numbers – ones and zeroes. So, something must happen in between you coding your program and the computer running it. And that something is a compiler.

A computer converts binary's ones and zeroes into on and off electrical signals to perform instructions.

A compiler converts programs written in a computer language into machine code – those ones and zeroes your computer understands. This is all done behind the scenes so that when you finish coding your program ...

... it's ready to run!

Why were early computers so BIG?

The first computers powered by electricity were built in the 1940s. They were mostly used for military maths like breaking secret codes or firing weapons accurately over long distances.

These early machines were **E-NOR-MOUS!**

ENIAC (**E**lectronic **N**umerical **I**ntegrator **A**nd **C**omputer) was a successful early US computer. All stretched out, it was 30 m long, 3 m high and weighed about 27 tonnes – the weight of six monster trucks.

I CAN'T BELIEVE THERE'S NO BUDGET LEFT FOR A STEPLADDER!

To run a new program, ENIAC was rewired by female staff called 'computers' (confusing, eh?). Rewiring to change to a new program could take two days!

10

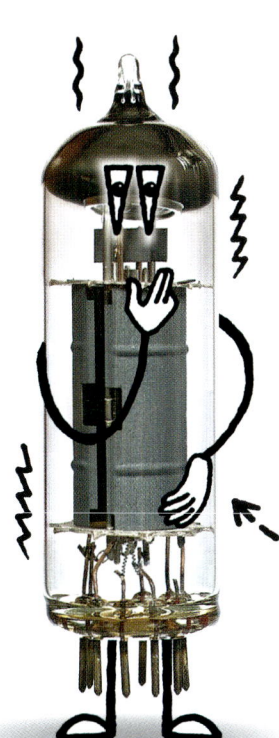

Why the weight?

Early electrical parts were bulky. ENIAC contained over 100,000 of them, as well as big bundles of wiring to connect them all. Among its parts were 17,468 vacuum tubes – large glass cylinders that acted as switches inside the computer.

Vacuum tubes got hot, broke down and consumed a LOT of power. ENIAC used 160,000 watts of electricity – about as much electricity as 13,300 iPads!

Vacuum tubes helped the machine perform logical tasks and make decisions.

WHY DID WE MAKE IT SO SMALL?

Tiny transistors

In 1947, three American scientists invented the transistor. This did the job of a vacuum tube, but far better. Transistors were more reliable, used less power and could be built a lot **SMALLER**.

Transistors and other electronic parts **SHRANK** further, and soon hundreds of transistors could be fitted to microscopic circuits set onto a fingernail-sized, thin wafer of silicon.
These were called integrated circuits or silicon chips.

Chips allowed smaller, faster and less power-hungry computers to be built. By 1997, US students shrank the giant ENIAC computer so that all its functions were performed by a single 8 mm by 5 mm silicon chip. Wow!

11

Why make microchips so tiny?

Silicon chips are titchy. **Building them so small makes it easier to fit chips inside small, portable devices.**

Did you know, for example, that many smartwatches cram not one but a dozen chips inside their slim cases?

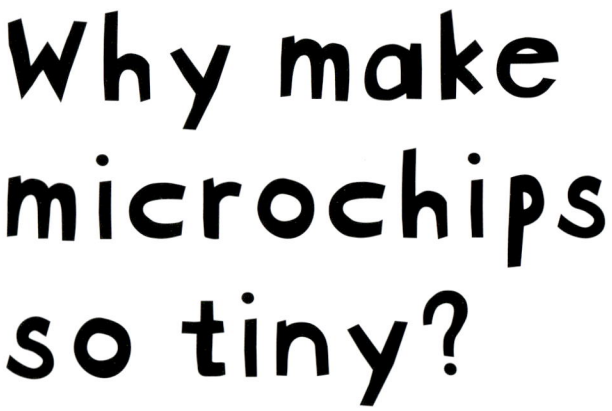

Smartwatch

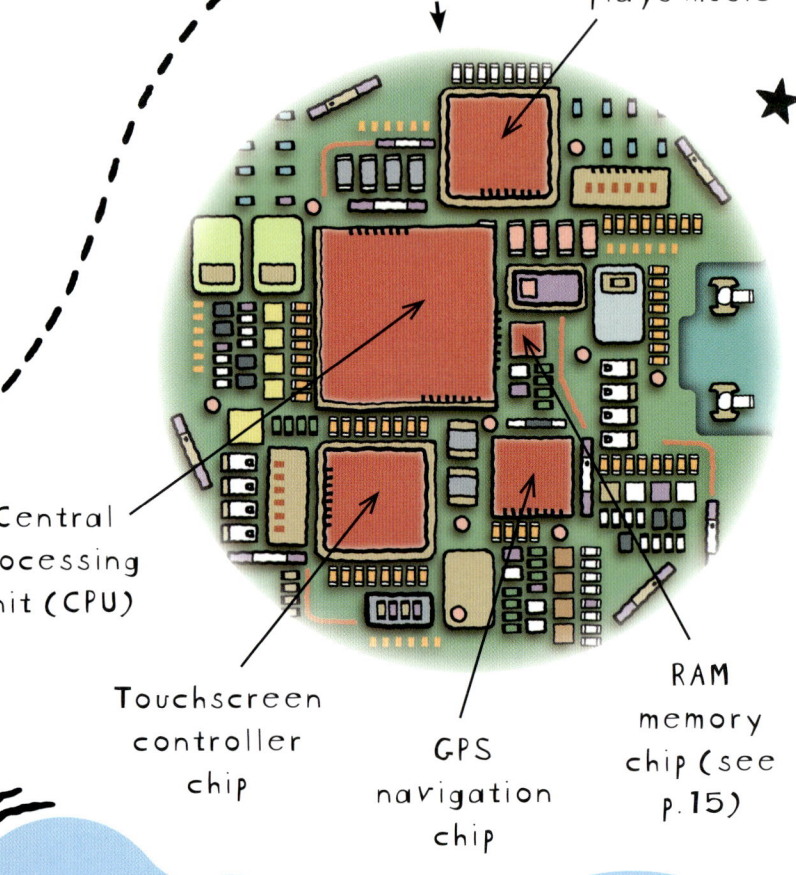

Sound chip plays music

Central processing unit (CPU)

Touchscreen controller chip

GPS navigation chip

RAM memory chip (see p.15)

TONIGHT USER, I HAVE MADE YOU SILI-CON CARNE!

Smart Pan 3000

Processing power

Microprocessors are chips that contain all the processing functions of an entire computer.

They're now found in all sorts of programmable devices and digital tech, from cars to kitchen appliances.

Small is beautiful

Keeping things small also saves materials and **INCREASES** speed. Electric signals whizz around the circuits of a chip. The less distance they have to travel between parts, the speedier the chip can operate.

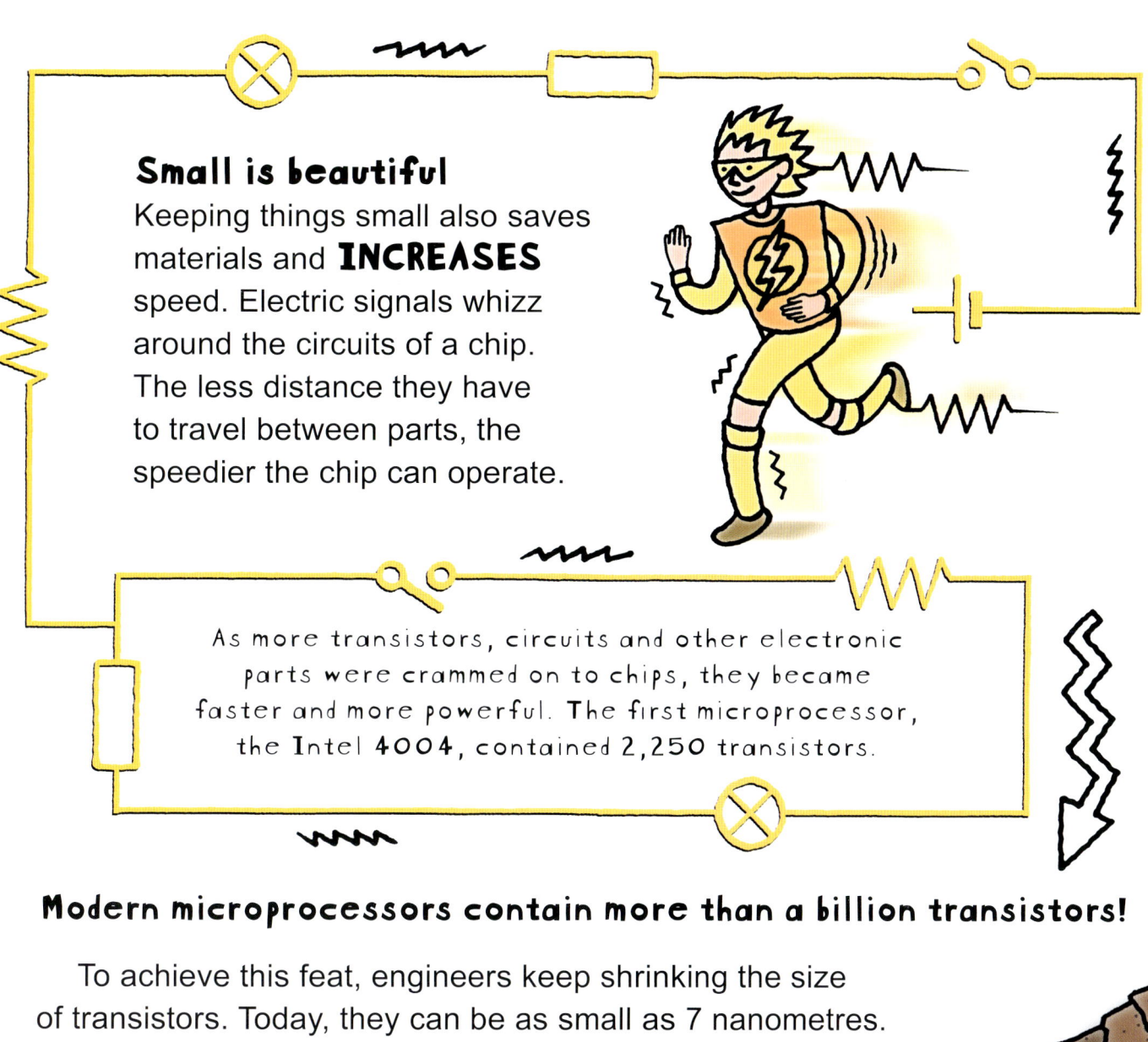

As more transistors, circuits and other electronic parts were crammed on to chips, they became faster and more powerful. The first microprocessor, the Intel 4004, contained 2,250 transistors.

Modern microprocessors contain more than a billion transistors!

To achieve this feat, engineers keep shrinking the size of transistors. Today, they can be as small as 7 nanometres. How small is that? Well, the average human hair is about 80 nanometres wide.

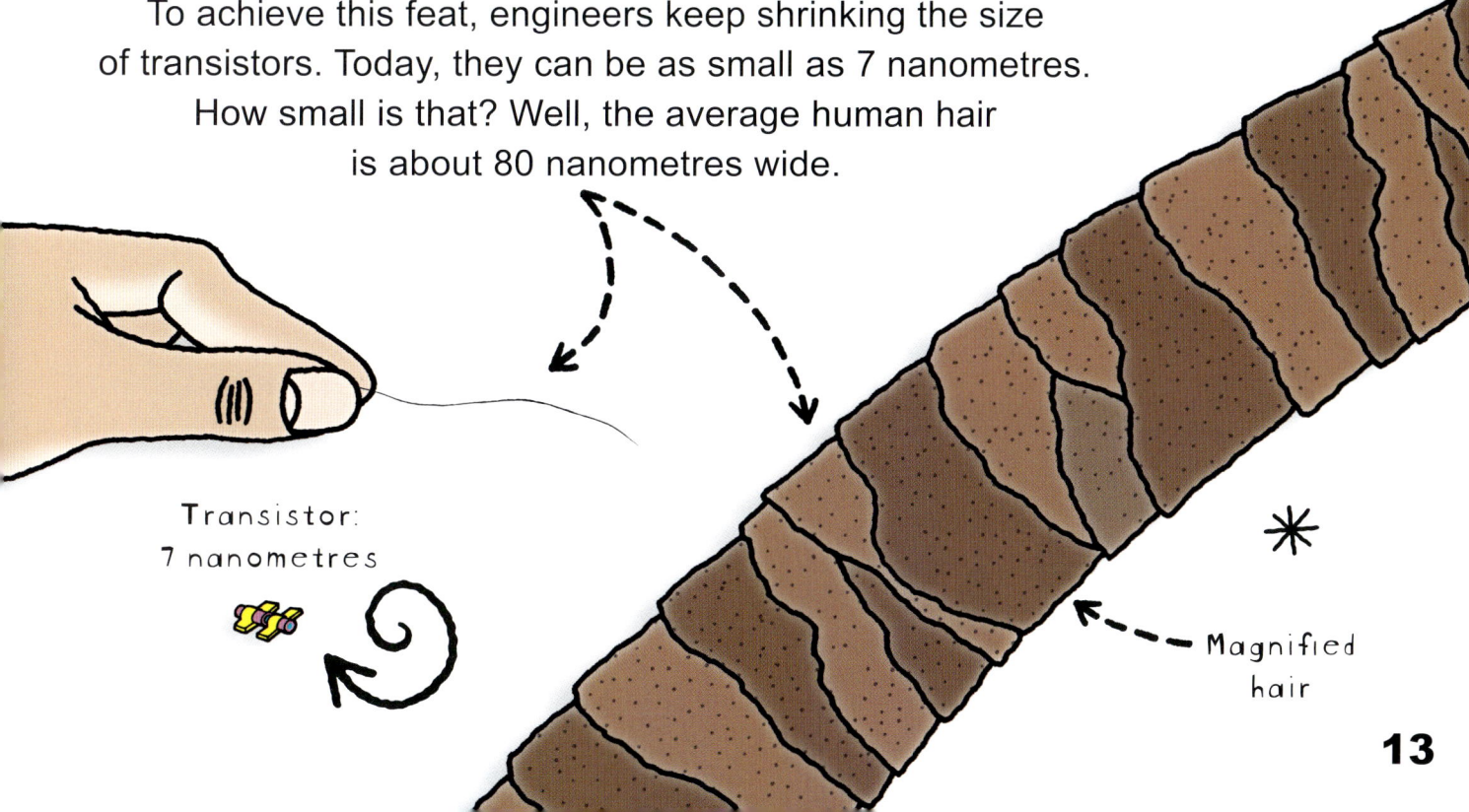

Transistor: 7 nanometres

Magnified hair

Where does all my data go?

When you save a cute pet picture, a tune you've written or an email you've typed, your computer or tablet stores it for later use. Most devices today use either flash memory or a hard disk drive to keep your data safe and secure.

Hard disk

A hard disk uses fast-spinning magnetic discs called platters to store files. When a new file is saved somewhere on the disc, its precise location is also stored in a file.

It's called the File Allocation Table or **FAT** for short. So when that file has to be found and opened later, the computer checks the FAT to know where it is!

The motor spins the spindle of metal discs round fast, up to 200 times a second.

The read/write head uses magnets to save data onto parts of one platter.

FAT acts like an address book, keeping track of where every file is stored.

The actuator arm travels in and out to reach all parts of the platters.

14

In a flash

Flash memory is amazing. It is 'solid state', meaning it has no moving parts. Instead, electric circuits store data, which stays stored when the computer is switched off.

Because it's much smaller, silent and uses less power than a hard drive, it's the storage of choice in small devices like smartphones and tablets.

RAM n' ROM

Computers also store programs and data in two types of memory. **ROM** (Read Only Memory) permanently holds programs and code used, for example, to start a computer.

SHHHHH!

SD card (mobile phones, digital cameras)

SSD memory (computers, tablets)

Pen drive (portable memory storage)

RAM (Random Access Memory) is used like scrap paper, as a temporary place to hold data while a computer is busy working. When the computer is switched off, all the data in **RAM** is lost.

Byte size

Measurements of memory all have the word 'bytes' in them. A kilobyte (KB) equals 1,024 bytes. Each measure up is 1,000 times bigger than the previous one.

(Except a nibble. A nibble is half a byte — seriously.)

I CAN STORE MORE THAN A MILLION MEGABYTES!

I'M 1,000 TIMES BIGGER THAN YOU.

I EQUAL 1,024 KILOBYTES.

15

Why do computers take soooo long to start?

When you press the start button on a computer, you can be in for a wait. Be patient; your machine's got a lot on its to-do list.

When power reaches your computer's CPU microprocessor, it leaps into action. It clears its own memory of any old data and sends signals to a ROM chip nearby.

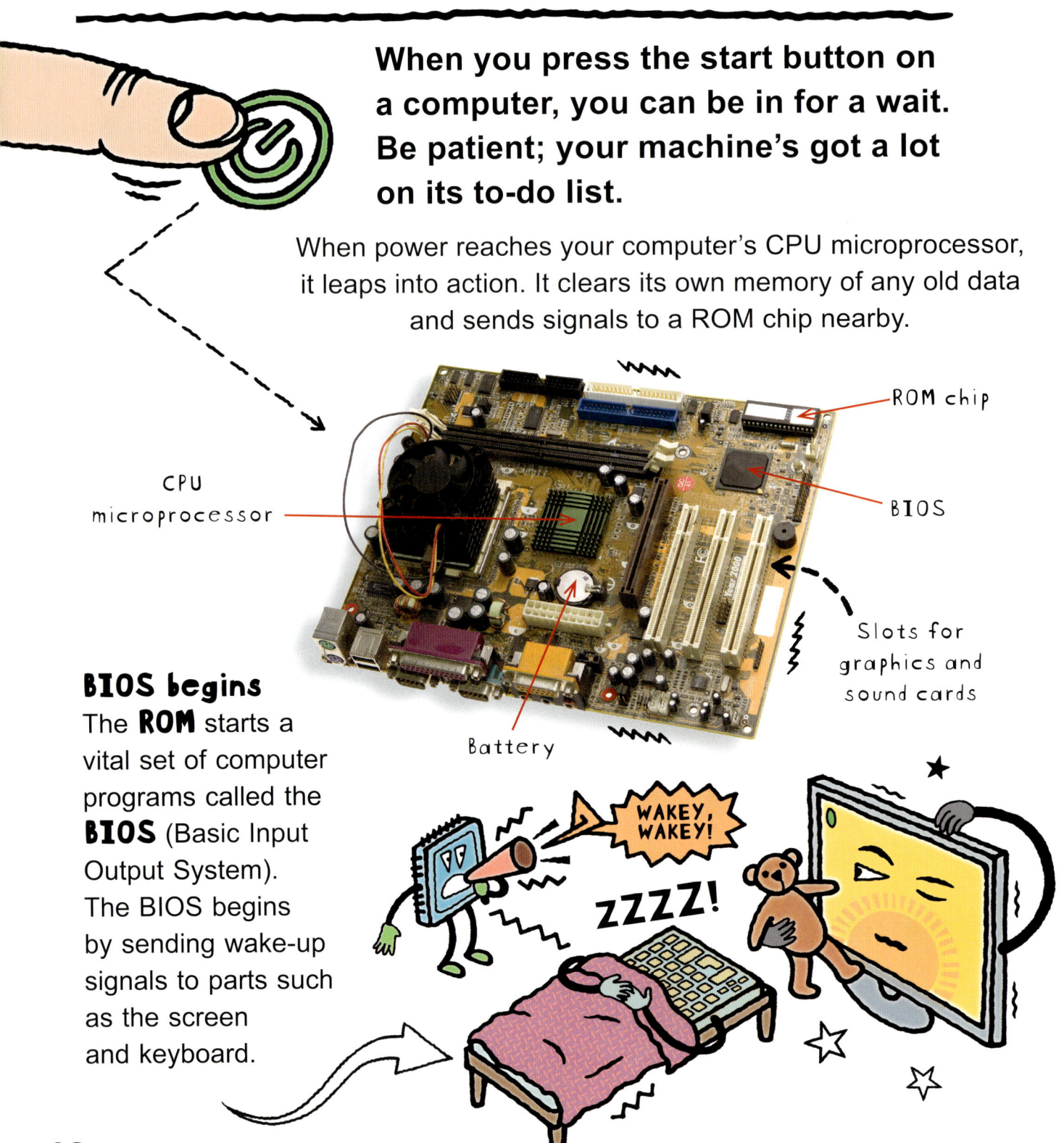

CPU microprocessor

ROM chip

BIOS

Slots for graphics and sound cards

Battery

BIOS begins
The **ROM** starts a vital set of computer programs called the **BIOS** (Basic Input Output System). The BIOS begins by sending wake-up signals to parts such as the screen and keyboard.

WAKEY, WAKEY!

ZZZZ!

Here's the POST
The BIOS works with the **CPU** to perform a **LOOOOONG** series of basic checks, known as **POST** – the Power-On Self-Test. The POST makes sure all the computer's key parts are there and working.

During POST, computers may click, whirr and lights flash as parts are checked thoroughly.

More to do
The hard disk is started, the computer's clock checked and ROM chips on other cards in the computer started so they can do their own start-up routines.

There's a lot going on!

Booting up
Once POST is completed, the BIOS hunts for the operating system, such as Android, Windows or iOS, and loads it into the computer's memory. This can take a little time as the operating system boots up and makes lots more checks itself.

IT'S ALL YOURS!

These are just some of the tasks performed before your computer is ready and raring to go!

Impatient at slow start-up? You're lucky you're not living in the 1950s. There was no BIOS on a ROM, you had to do all the checks yourself. They could take hours!

17

How does what I type reach the screen?

Good question.

When you type 'My dog smells' or something else on a keyboard, it appears almost instantly on the screen. In the split-second between those two events, a lot occurs …

A microprocessor built into the keyboard is constantly on the lookout for a change in the electric signals passing around the keyboard's circuits.

Keyboard warrior

As a key is pressed down, its spring squeezes together and two sets of electrical contacts touch. These complete an electrical circuit.

Scan codes and interrupts

The microprocessor generates a two-digit number unique to each key, called a scan code. It sends this to the computer for the BIOS (see previous page) to read. It also sends an interrupt signal straight to the CPU, telling it to drop everything and focus on the scan code.

18

MY DOG SMELLS TAP!

Which program?
The CPU might be running a dozen different programs at any time. It drops everything for a tiny moment and works with the operating system to figure out which program was being used when the key was pressed.

My · dog · smells #
My·dog·smells #
My · dog · smells #

If the key was pressed in a word processing program, the operating system must display the character in the font selected by the user.

On screen
The scan code is converted into the correct character, which is sent to the computer's graphics processor. This sends the character as a signal that can be displayed on the screen.

Type test

How fast can you type? Get a friend to time you for 120 seconds as you type out as much of a page of a book as you can. Count only the words you typed correctly and divide by two to get your WPM — words per minute.

10-20 WPM is fine, 30 WPM is awesome! The fewer mistakes, the better.

 The fastest ever typer was Stella Pajunas-Garnand. She managed an incredible

216 WPM!

She set this record in 1946, on a typewriter.

19

How do computer games know the score?

You're moving up the levels, zapping baddies out of your way. On the screen are your vital gaming statistics – your total score and the number of lives left. But how does your computer keep track?

Score store

A computer game is a program and all programs rely on variables to work. Each variable is a small store of data that the program can access and change while it runs. Coders create variables in their programs and give (or assign) each variable a starting value.

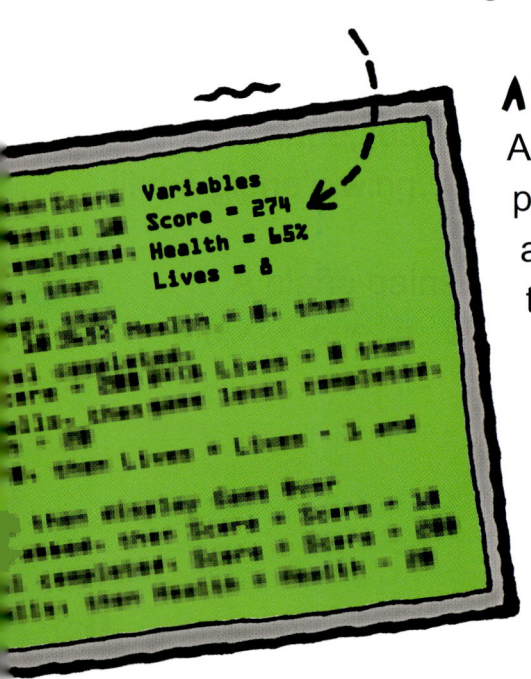

Variables
Score = 274
Health = 65%
Lives = 8

All change

As the game progresses, the program code registers each time an event occurs. It returns to the variables and changes them according to the game's rules. So, for example, when a player performs certain actions that win them points, the program adds those points ...

GO TO THE TOP OF PAGE 21!

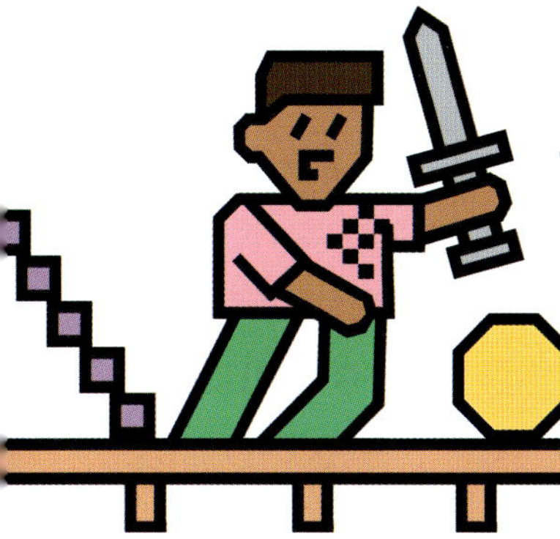

... to the Score variable.

If gold coin grabbed, then Score = Score + 10

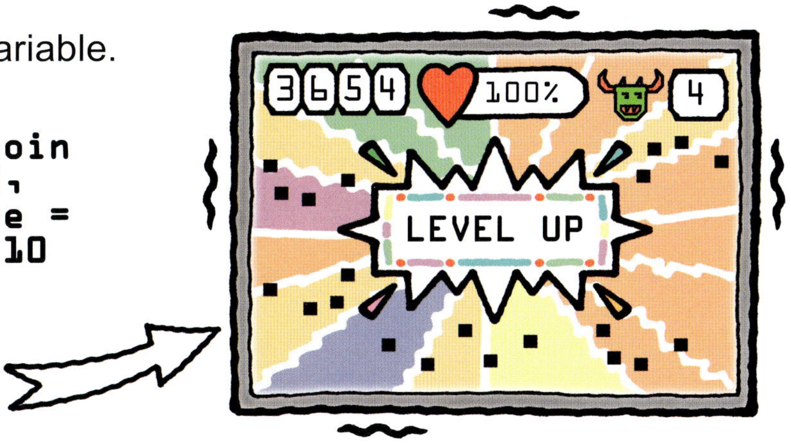

3654
100%
4
LEVEL UP

If game level completed, then Score = Score + 200

Keeping track

Variables keep note of failure and success in a game. In this example, each piece of misfortune the gamer suffers leads to the Health variable being reduced.

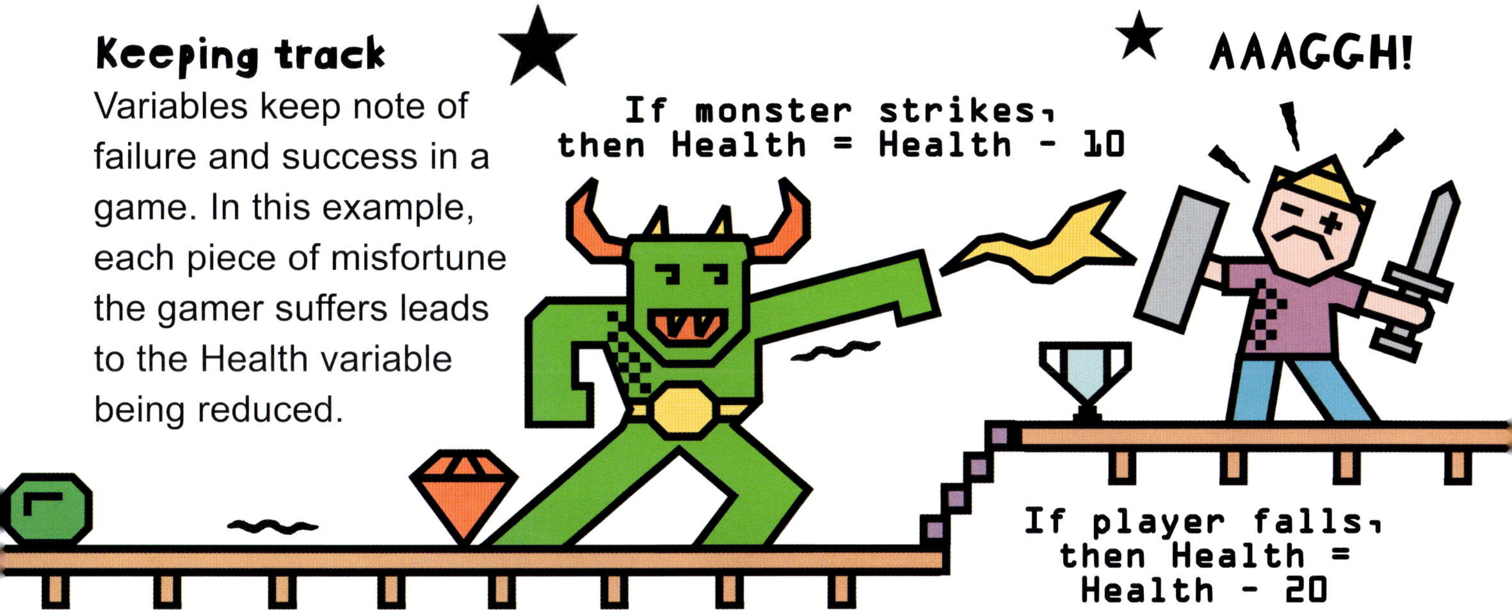

AAAGGH!
If monster strikes, then Health = Health - 10
If player falls, then Health = Health - 20

Decisions, decisions

The game program may make decisions based on a variable's value. If the Health variable reaches zero, then according to the game's rules, the player loses a life. The program has to remove 1 from the Life variable, reset the Health variable to 100 and check whether losing a life ends the game.

If Health = 0, then Lives = Lives - 1 and Health = 100
8941
0%
9
GAME OVER
If Lives = 0 then display Game Over

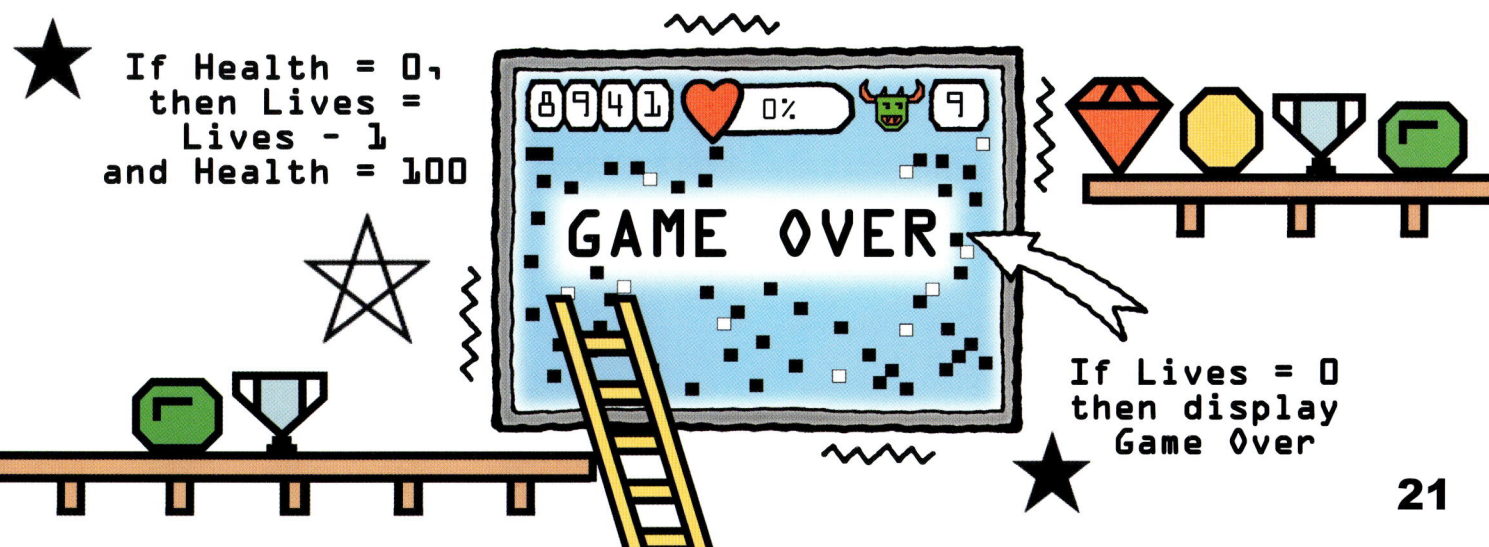

Is a bug the same as a virus?

We all make mistakes. So, don't be too hard on others (or yourself) if a program doesn't work quite as it should. Errors in programs are known as bugs.

Sometimes, they're simple spelling mistakes. Just occasionally, they can be disastrous. Bugs have caused an unmanned space rocket to blow up and a Mars spacecraft to miss its target.

Patch it up
When a bug is found in a program, users can download a small additional program, called a fix, or patch, to sort out the problem.

Computer viruses
Bugs are accidental, but viruses are deliberate. These are code designed to harm your computer's performance. Viruses may slow computers down, erase data or lock you out from your machine.

Terrifying!

Viruses are found in some files downloaded from the Internet or in email attachments. They can copy themselves and spread to other programs and even connected computers.

Other nasties

Viruses are one of several threats to your computer's security – together known as

malware.

Spyware are programs that steal personal information such as passwords, your email address book and even bank account details.

Trojan horses appear to be useful programs, but they can also steal personal data.

A worm is code that can make dozens of copies of itself on a computer, slowing or shutting it down.

Stay Safe: Top Tips

Get an adult to check the computer is running up-to-date anti-virus software.

Only download data from trusted sites and with permission from a parent or carer.

Use strong passwords and change them regularly.

Don't open unknown files.

23

Could a laser printer destroy the world?

Lasers are concentrated beams of light. You've probably seen them in sci-fi movies zapping cities or blowing up spacecraft. Laser printers contain lasers, so why aren't we more worried?

Some lasers are powerful enough to cut through sheet metal, but zapping cities is pure fantasy. And the laser inside a laser printer is really small and harmless. It does perform an important job in printing, though.

Printing with lasers

When you send a document to a printer, its processor splits it up into all the little dots that need to be printed. The laser then beams these patterns of dots onto a cylinder called a **DRUM**. The places on the drum where the laser's light strikes gain a negative charge of static electricity.

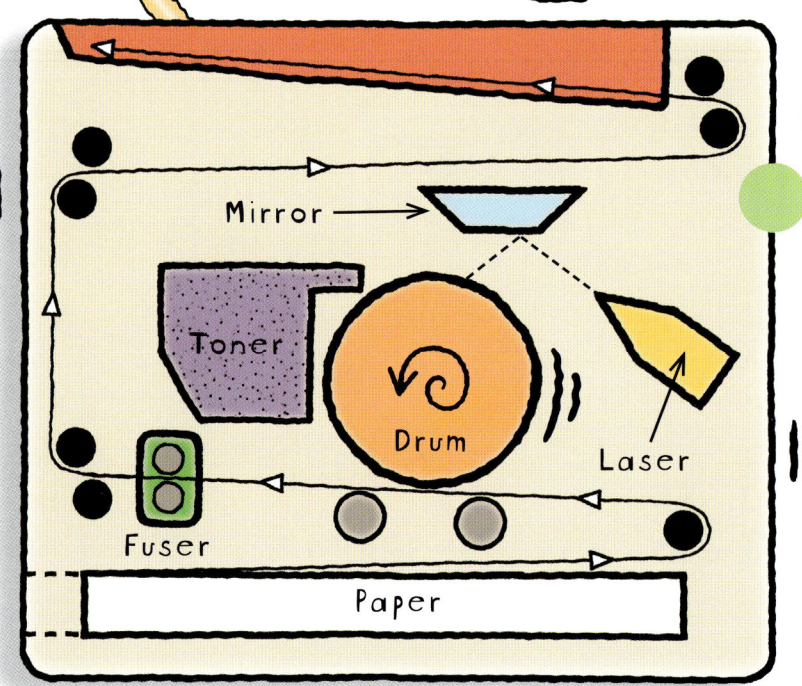

Laser printer

Static electricity

If you rub a balloon on a woolly jumper, it builds up a charge of static electricity. The balloon becomes negatively charged and will be attracted to things with a positive charge, like a wall.

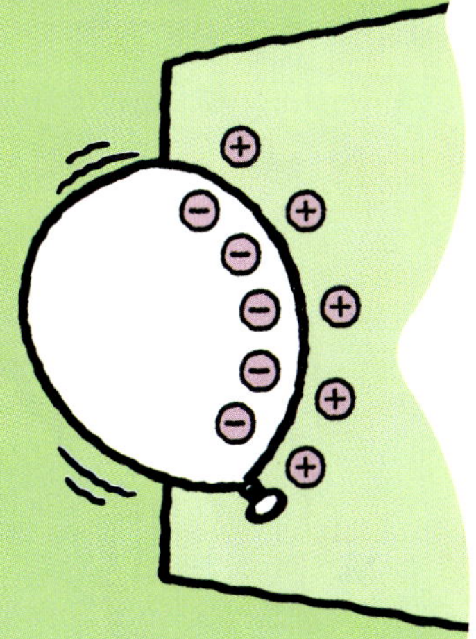

Place the charged balloon near your head for a hair-raising moment!

Powder power

Toner is a fine plastic powder that is given a positive electric charge. It's applied to the printer drum but only sticks to the parts of the drum that have a negative charge, because **POSITIVE AND NEGATIVE CHARGES ATTRACT**.

Once covered in toner, the drum turns. It transfers the toner on to paper that has been given an opposite electric charge to the toner. Clever!

As a result, the toner sticks to the paper, printing the image or text on to the page.

Hot off the press

The last stage of the printing process is red-hot. The printed page is heated briefly up to 150-215°C by a part called the **FUSER**. This makes the toner melt and stick to the page. Within moments, a completed page travels out of the printer, still warm to the touch.

MMM, TOASTY!

25

What's so super about supercomputers?

A lot of things.

These mega machines are super-large, super-powerful and super-fast. And super-expensive. The 2020 Fugaku supercomputer from Japan, for example, cost about £740 million!

In 1976, the Cray 1, an early supercomputer, cost about as much as 60 houses.

How large?

Supercomputers sprawl across giant rooms, sometimes the size of two or more tennis courts. They may contain 30,000 times more memory than your computer at home.

A regular computer tends to have just one CPU — the silicon chip that performs calculations and bosses all the other parts.

Supercomputers have a lot more. Fugaku, for example, has 158,976 CPUs!

Splitting stuff up

A regular computer tackles each task methodically, one stage at a time. This is called **serial processing**.

A supercomputer works more quickly by splitting tasks into little pieces and using all its processors to work on the pieces at the same time. This is called **parallel processing** and it's fast!

How fast?

Most modern supercomputers are at least **one million times faster** than your home computer. China's Sunway TaihuLight supercomputer can make a mind-numbing 93,000 billion calculations a second – that's **58 million times faster** than an iPad 2.

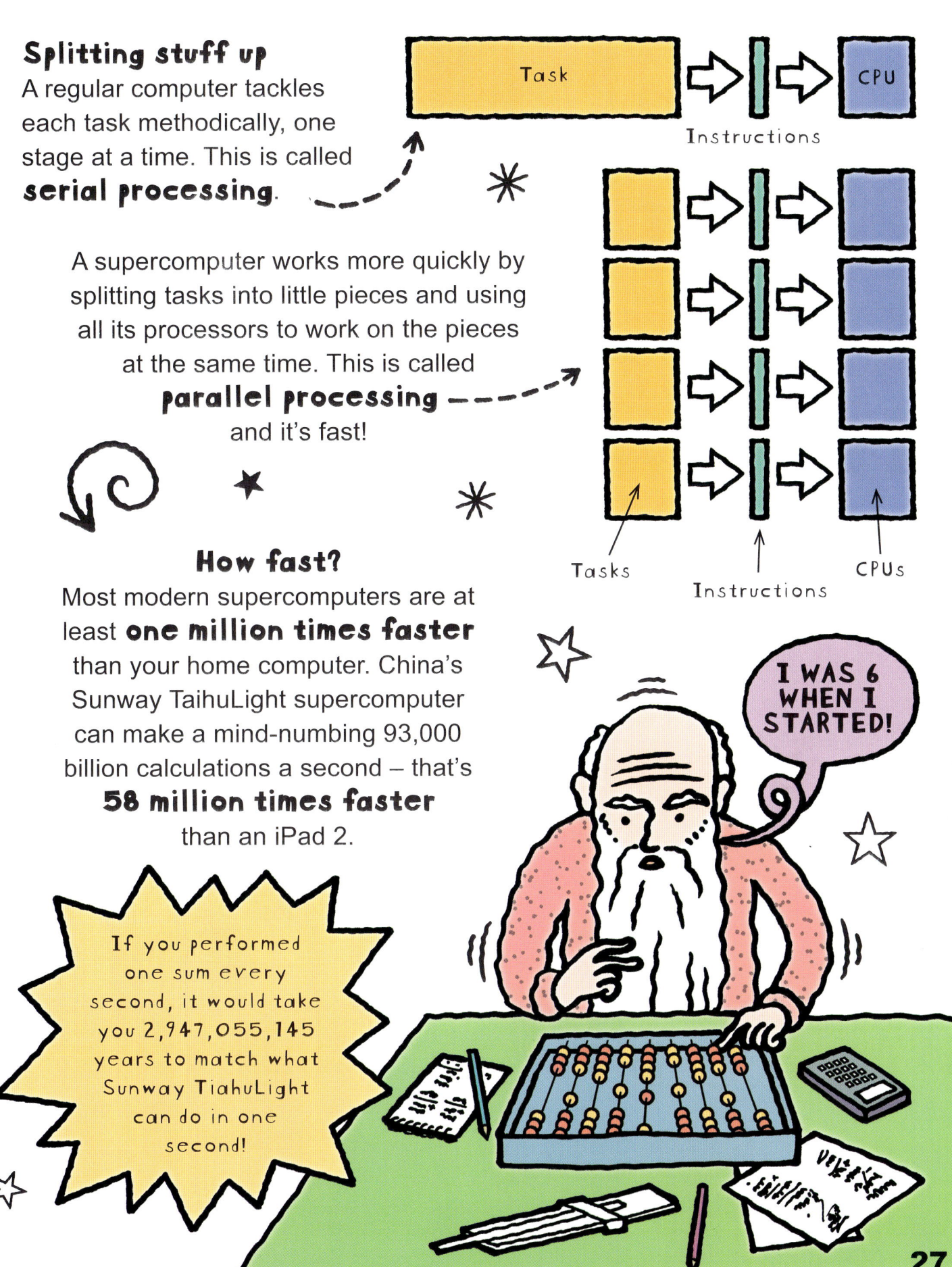

I WAS 6 WHEN I STARTED!

If you performed one sum every second, it would take you 2,947,055,145 years to match what Sunway TiahuLight can do in one second!

Quick-fire questions

Why is a mouse called a mouse?

Back in 1964, Americans Douglas Engelbart and Bill English built a wooden box to move a cursor across a computer screen. They first called it an 'X-Y Position Indicator for a display system' – not the snappiest title. Thankfully, the box's long cable looked a little like a mouse's tail and the name 'mouse' stuck instead.

What's the difference between Bluetooth and WiFi?

Only one of these is named after a legendary Viking warrior (clue: it isn't WiFi). Both, though, use radio transmitters to send data between different devices without wires. Bluetooth works over short distances (up to 10 m) between two devices that are paired. WiFi works over longer distances and connects computers and other devices to the Internet.

Why must I backup my data?

Backups can be a drag, but they're important to do. Technology is amazing, but sometimes it goes wrong. A computer can be infected by a virus, while portable tech can be lost or dropped and broken. Backing up your important files keeps them safe if your tech suffers a problem.

Are there really buses inside my computer?

You bet! A bus is the technical term for a connection between different computer parts that transfers data between the two. When you plug a mouse or some other device into a USB (**U**niversal **S**erial **B**us) port, a bus helps signals travel between the mouse and the computer. Think of buses dropping off data like real buses do passengers!

How do I create strong passwords?

By using random collections of different characters including upper and lower case letters, as well as numbers and punctuation marks like $ and *. Keep your passwords hard to guess by not using key words about you, such as the name of your pet or favourite band.

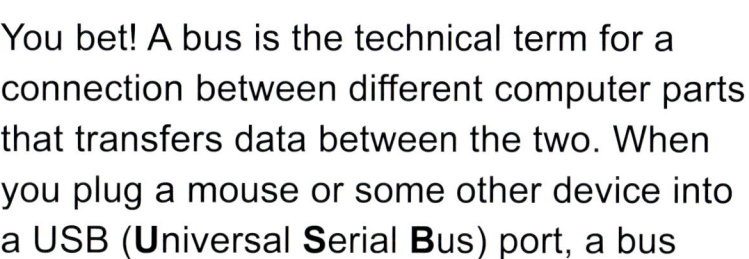

29

Glossary

App A small computer program, such as a game, that can be downloaded and used on tablets, smartphones and other mobile devices.

Bug An error or fault in the code of a computer program that produces an unexpected or unwanted result.

Circuit A path along which an electric signal travels. A circuit can be made of wires or set on to parts of a silicon chip.

Compiler A computer program that converts another program, written in a programming language, into code that a computer can act upon.

CPU (Central Processing Unit) A powerful series of electronic circuits (usually in a microprocessor) that perform all the calculations in a computer and control the computer's parts.

Cursor A moving symbol, such as an arrow or flashing block, that shows a position on a computer's screen.

Download When you copy information that is located on another computer to your own computer, such as when you download a free game from the Internet.

Font A collection of letters, numbers and other characters all in the same style.

Gigabyte (GB) A measure of memory. One gigabyte equals 1,024 megabytes (MB) and 1,024 gigabytes equals one terabyte (TB).

Internet A giant computer network of smaller computer networks that allows people to send, receive and share data with one another.

Malware Programs and computer code designed to harm your computer or steal your personal data.

Memory Part of a computer or other digital device in which information can be stored for later use.

Microprocessor A complete computing unit on a single chip that can perform thousands or millions of operations per second.

Network Two or more computers or digital devices that are linked so that they can communicate with one another.

Operating system Computer programs that run a computer's basic functions and manage other programs running on the system.

Peripheral Any external device attached to a computer, such as a printer, mouse, keyboard or scanner.

RAM (Random Access Memory) A type of computer memory that can store information and be rewritten while the computer is running.

ROM (Read Only Memory) A type of permanent memory that doesn't lose data when the computer is switched off.

Transistor Tiny parts that act as switches and amplifiers in computers and other electronic circuits.

Variable A named place for storing information in a computer program.

Virus A harmful program that can copy itself to spread from one computer to another.

WiFi Wireless network technology that allows people to connect computers and other digital devices to each other and the Internet.

Further reading

Websites

www.bbc.co.uk/bitesize/topics/zs7s4wx
Lots of clear, short articles and videos on data, computer networks and programming.

www.techradar.com/uk/news/computing/the-10-most-influential-computers-in-history-707891
Meet the abacus and nine famous computers that had a major impact on the world of computing.

www.youtube.com/watch?v=DKGZ1aPlVLY
A great video by Code.org explaining computer processing and storage.

www.youtube.com/watch?v=HB4I2CgkcCo
Check out all the key parts of most computer systems in this short, but useful, video.

www.computerhope.com/history/
Dozens of short, handy timelines of computer history about processors, computer games and much more.

Books

A World of Computers and Coding
by Clive Gifford (Wayland, 2019)

How Super Cool Tech Works
(DK, 2020)

The Thrilling Adventures of Babbage and Lovelace
by Sydney Padua (Penguin, 2016)

100 Things To Know About Numbers, Computers and Coding
by Alice James et al (Usborne, 2018)

Every effort has been made by the Publishers to ensure that the websites in this book are suitable for children, that they are of the highest educational value, and that they contain no inappropriate or offensive material. However, because of the nature of the Internet, it is impossible to guarantee that the contents of these sites will not be altered. We strongly advise that Internet access is supervised by a responsible adult.

Index

A
Analytical Engine 7

B
Babbage, Charles 6–8
backup (data) 29
binary 9
BIOS (Basic Input Output System) 16–18
Bluetooth 28
bug 22
bus (see also 'USB') 29
bytes 15

C
calculation 4, 6–7, 26–27
chips (computer) see also 'microchips' 6, 11–13, 16–17, 26
code 8–9, 15, 18– 20, 22–23
coders 8–9, 20
coding languages 9
compilers 4, 9
computers (ENIAC staff) 10
CPU (Central Processing Unit) 12, 16–19, 26–27, 29

D
data 4–5, 14–16, 20, 22–23, 28–29
Difference Engine 6–7
download 22–23

E
electricity 6, 10–11, 24–25
electricity, static 24–25
email 4, 14, 23
ENIAC 10–11

F
FAT (File Allocation Table) 14
flash memory 5, 14–15
Fugaku 26

G
games (computer) 8, 20–21
Gates, Bill 5

H
hard disc 14, 17
hardware 4
Hopper, Grace 4

I
input 4
Internet 23, 28

K
keyboards 4, 16, 18

L
laser 4
Lovelace (Countess of), Ada 8

M
malware 23
memory 5, 7, 12, 14–17, 26
microchips 12–13
microprocessors 12–13, 16, 18
Microsoft 5
motherboard 29
mouse 28–29

N
nibbles (unit of memory) 15

O
operating systems 8, 17, 19
output 4

P
Pajunas-Garnand, Stella 19
password 23, 29
pen drive 5, 15
POST (Power-On Self-Test) 17
printer 24–25
processing 4, 12, 19, 27
processing, parallel 27
processing, serial 27
processor 7, 19, 24, 27
programs 4, 7–10, 13, 15–16, 19–23
programming 4, 8

R
RAM (Random Access Memory) 12, 15
ROM (Read Only Memory) 15–17

S
safety 23
scan code 18–19
screens (see also 'touch-screens) 4, 16, 18–19, 20, 28
SD card 15
silicon 6, 11–12, 26
smartphones 4–5, 8, 15
smartwatches 12
software 4–5, 23
spyware 23
SSD 15
Sunway TaihuLight 27
supercomputers 26–27

T
touchscreens 4, 12
transistors 11, 13
Trojan horse 23
Turing, Alan 5
type 14, 18–19

U
USB (Universal Serial Bus) 29

V
vacuum tubes 11
variable 20–21
virus 22–23, 29

W
WiFi 28
worm 23

32